LEADER'S GUIDE

PREPARING

for the

GLORY

Other Books by John & Carol Arnott

Preparing for The Glory

Manifestations and Prophetic Symbolism

From Here to the Nations: The Story of the Toronto Blessing

The Invitation

Grace and Forgiveness

Experience the Blessing

The Father's Blessing

PREPARING

for the

GLORY

*Getting Ready for the Next Wave
of Holy Spirit Outpouring*

JOHN & CAROL ARNOTT

Leader's Guide prepared by Larry Sparks

DESTINY IMAGE® PUBLISHERS, INC.
P.O. Box 310, Shippensburg, PA 17257-0310
"Promoting Inspired Lives."

This book and all other Destiny Image and Destiny Image Fiction books are available at Christian bookstores and distributors worldwide.

Interior design by Terry Clifton

For more information on foreign distributors, call 717-532-3040.
Reach us on the Internet: www.destinyimage.com.

ISBN 13: 978-0-7684-1793-7
Ebook 13 ISBN: 978-0-7684-4304-2

For Worldwide Distribution, Printed in the U.S.A.
1 2 3 4 5 6 7 8 /21 20 19 18

CONTENT

HELLO!

We want to thank you for partnering with us in leading our new course, *Preparing for the Glory*. We envision this course as an opportunity to prepare others for the power of God that we have so profoundly experienced. It is our desire to equip leaders who have also been ignited in revival to lead others to Him in this way as well.

Over the course of the next eight weeks, you will equip your group as they discover what it means to be anointed of the Lord, how to steward His presence and glory in their own lives, and why it's so important to walk in holiness and honor as they pursue the things of God. It is our hope that through leading this course, you will find a renewed passion to empower those around you as they seek revival.

Thank you again for taking the time to be with us. We are praying for you as you lead your group toward the glory of God!

Blessings,

John and Carol Arnott

BASIC LEADER GUIDELINES

This study is designed to help you develop into a believer who can cultivate, sustain and carry revival wherever you go. From *this* perspective, you will partner with God to see impossibilities bow at Jesus' name and step into the destiny God has for you!

There are several different ways that you can engage this study. These are the standard outlets recommended to facilitate this curriculum. We encourage you to seek the Lord's direction, be creative, and prepare for supernatural transformation in your Christian life.

When all is said and done, this curriculum is unique in that the end goal is *not* information—it is transformation. The sessions are intentionally sequenced to take every believer on a journey from information, to revelation, to transformation. Participants will receive a greater understanding of what partnership with Heaven looks like and learn how to practically live this supernatural lifestyle on a daily basis.

Here are some of the ways you can use the curriculum:

1. CHURCH SMALL GROUP

Often churches feature a variety of different small group opportunities per season in terms of books, curriculum resources, and Bible studies. *Preparing for the Glory* would be included among the offering of titles for whatever season you are launching for the small group program.

It is recommended that you have at least four to five people to make up a small group and a maximum of twelve.

For a small group setting, here are the essentials:

- *Meeting place*: Either the leader's home or a space provided by the church.

- *Appropriate technology*: A DVD player attached to a TV that is large enough for all of the group members to see (and loud enough for everyone to hear).

- *Leader/Facilitator*: This person will often be the host, if the small group is being conducted at someone's home; but it can also be a team (husband/wife, two church leaders, etc.). The leader(s) will direct the session from beginning to end, from sending reminder e-mails to participating group members about the meetings, to closing out the sessions in prayer and dismissing everyone. A detailed description of what the group meetings should look like will follow in the pages to come.

Sample Schedule for Home Group Meeting (for a 7:00 P.M. Meeting)

- Before arrival: Ensure that refreshments are ready by 6:15 P.M. If they need to be refrigerated, ensure they are preserved appropriately until 15 minutes prior to the official meeting time.

- 6:15 P.M.: Leaders arrive at meeting home or facility.

- 6:15–6:25 P.M.: Connect with hosts, co-hosts, and/or co-leaders to review the evening's program.

- 6:25–6:35 P.M.: Pray with hosts, co-hosts, and/or co-leaders for the evening's events. Here are some sample prayer directives:

  - For the Holy Spirit to move and minister freely.

  - For the teaching to connect with and transform all who hear it.

  - For dialogue and conversation that edifies and is transparent among the group members.

  - For the presence of God to manifest through testimonies and answered prayers.

  - For increased hunger for God's presence and power.

- 6:35–6:45: Ensure technology is functioning properly!

  - Test the DVDs featuring the teaching sessions, making sure they are set up to the appropriate session.

- If you are doing praise and worship, ensure that either the MP3 player or CD player is functional, set at an appropriate volume and that lyrics are available for everyone to sing along.

- 6:45–7:00 p.m.: Welcome and greeting for guests.

- 7:00–7:10 p.m.: Fellowship, community, and refreshments.

- 7:10–7:30 p.m.: Introductory prayer and worship.

- 7:30–7:40 p.m.: Ministry and prayer time.

- 7:40–8:00 p.m.: Watch DVD session.

- 8:00–8:20 p.m.: Discuss DVD session.

- 8:20–8:35 p.m.: Activation time.

- 8:35–8:40 p.m.: Closing prayer and dismiss.

This sample schedule is *not* intended to lock you into a formula. It is simply provided as a template to help you get started. Our hope is that you customize it according to the unique needs of your group and sensitively navigate the activity of the Holy Spirit as He uses these sessions to supernaturally transform the lives of every person participating in the study.

2. SMALL GROUP CHURCH-WIDE CAMPAIGN

This would be the decision of the pastor or senior leadership of the church. In this model, the entire church would go through *Preparing for the Glory* in both the main services and ancillary small groups/life classes.

The pastor's weekend sermon would be based on the principles in *Preparing for the Glory*, and the Sunday school classes/life classes and/or small groups would also follow the *Preparing for the Glory* curriculum format.

3. CHURCH CLASS | MIDWEEK CLASS | SUNDAY SCHOOL CURRICULUM

Churches of all sizes offer a variety of classes to develop members into more effective disciples of Jesus and agents of transformation in their spheres of influence.

Preparing for the Glory would be an invaluable addition to a church's class offering. Typically, churches offer a variety of topical classes targeted at men's needs, women's needs, marriage, family, finances, and various areas of Bible study.

4. INDIVIDUAL STUDY

While the curriculum is designed for use in a group setting, it also works as a tool that can equip anyone who is looking to strengthen his or her spirit and soul.

STEPS TO LAUNCHING A *PREPARING FOR THE GLORY* GROUP OR CLASS

PREPARE WITH PRAYER!

Pray! If you are a **church leader**, prayerfully consider how *Preparing for the Glory* could transform the culture and climate of your church community! Spend some time with the Holy Spirit, asking Him to give you vision for what this unique study will do for your church, and ultimately, how a Kingdom-minded people will transform your city and region.

If you are a **group leader** or **class facilitator**, pray for those who will be attending your group, signing up for your class, and will be positioning their lives to be transformed by the power and presence of God in this study.

PREPARE PRACTICALLY!

Determine how you will be using the Preparing for the Glory curriculum.

Identify which of the following formats you will be using the curriculum in:

- Church-sponsored small group study

- Church-wide campaign

- Church class (Wednesday night, Sunday morning, etc.)

- Individual study

Determine a meeting location and ensure availability of appropriate equipment.

Keep in mind the number of people who may attend. You will also need AV (audio-visual) equipment. The more comfortable the setting, the more people will enjoy being there, and will spend more time ministering to each other!

A word of caution here: the larger the group, the greater the need for co-leaders or assistants. The ideal small group size is difficult to judge; however, once you get more than ten to twelve people, it becomes difficult for each member to feel "heard." If your group is larger than 12 people, consider either having two or more small group discussion leaders or "multiplying" the larger group into two smaller ones.

Determine the format for your meetings.

The presence of the Lord, which brings transformation, is cradled and stewarded well in the midst of organization. Structure should never replace spontaneity; on the contrary, having a plan and determining what type of format your meetings will take enables you to flow with the Holy Spirit and minister more effectively.

Set a schedule for your meetings.

Once you have established the format for your meetings, set a schedule for your meetings. Some groups like to have a time of fellowship or socializing (either before or after the meeting begins) where light refreshments are offered. Some groups will want to incorporate times of worship and personal ministry into the small group or class. This is highly recommended for *Preparing for the Glory*, as the study is designed to be founded upon equipping and activating believers through encountering God's presence. The video portion and discussion questions are intended to instruct believers, while the worship, times of ministry, group interaction, prayer time, and activation elements are purposed to engage them to live out what they just learned.

Establish a start date along with a weekly meeting day and time.

This eight-week curriculum should be followed consistently and consecutively. Be mindful of the fact that while there are eight weeks of material, most groups will want to meet one last time after completing the last week to celebrate, or designate their first meeting as a time to get to know each other and "break the ice." This is very normal and should be encouraged to continue the community momentum that the small group experience initiates. Typically, after the final session is completed, groups will often engage in a social activity—either going out to dinner together, seeing a movie, or something of the like.

Look far enough ahead on the calendar to account for anything that might interfere. Choose a day that works well for the members of your group.

Advertise!

Getting the word out in multiple ways is most effective. Print out flyers, post a sign-up sheet, make an announcement in church services or group meetings, send out weekly e-mails and text messages, set up your own blog or website, or post the event on the social media avenue you and your group use most (Facebook, Twitter, etc.). A personal invitation or phone call is a great way to reach those who might need that little bit of extra encouragement to get involved.

Gather your materials.

Each leader will need the *Preparing for the Glory* Leader's Kit, as well as the *Preparing for the Glory* book.

Additionally, each participant will need a personal copy of the *Essential Training for Preparing for the Glory* study guide. It is recommended they also purchase the *Preparing for the Glory* book for further enrichment and as a resource to complement their daily readings. However, they are able to engage in the exercises and participate in the group discussion apart from reading the book.

We have found it best for the materials to all be purchased at one time—many booksellers and distributors offer discounts on multiple orders, and you are assured that each member will have their materials from the beginning of the course.

STEP FORWARD!

Arrive at your meeting in *plenty* of time to prepare. Nametags are a great idea, at least for the first couple of meetings. Icebreaker and introduction activities are also a good idea for the first meeting.

Pray for your members. As much as possible, make yourself available to them. Embrace the journey that you and your fellow members are embarking on; transformation begins within *you*!

THANK YOU

Thank you for embarking on a journey to equip the body of Christ to be empowered to carry and sustain revival in their lives and communities.

LEADER CHECKLIST

ONE TO TWO MONTHS PRIOR

_____ Have you determined a start date for your class or small group?

_____ Have you determined the format, meeting day and time, and weekly meeting schedule?

_____ Have you selected a meeting location (making sure you have adequate space and AV equipment available)?

_____ Have you advertised? Do you have a sign-up sheet to ensure you order enough materials?

THREE WEEKS TO ONE MONTH PRIOR

_____ Have you ordered materials? You will need a copy of *Preparing for the Glory* Leader's Kit, along with copies of the study guide and book for each participant.

_____ Have you organized your meeting schedule/format?

ONE TO TWO WEEKS PRIOR

_____ Have you received all your materials?

_____ Have you reviewed the DVDs and your Leader's Kit to familiarize yourself with the material and to ensure everything is in order?

_____ Have you planned and organized the refreshments, if you are planning to provide them? Some leaders will handle this themselves, and some find it easier to allow participants to sign up to provide refreshments if they would like to do so.

_____ Have you advertised and promoted? This includes sending out e-mails to all participants, setting up a Facebook group, promotion in the church bulletin, etc.

_____ Have you appointed co-leaders to assist you with the various portions of the group/class?

FIRST MEETING DAY

_____ Plan to arrive *early!* Give yourself extra time to set up the meeting space, double-check all AV equipment, and organize your materials. It might be helpful to ask participants to arrive 15 minutes early for the first meeting to allow for distribution of materials and any icebreaker activity you might have planned.

Session Discussion Questions:
WEEKLY OVERVIEW
OF MEETINGS/GROUP
SESSIONS

Here are some instructions on how to use each of the weekly Discussion Question guides.

WELCOME AND FELLOWSHIP TIME *(10–15 Minutes)*

This usually begins five to ten minutes prior to the designated meeting time and typically continues up until ten minutes after the official starting time. Community is important. One of the issues in many small group/class environments is the lack of connectivity among the people.

Welcome: Greet everyone as they walk in. If it is a small group environment, as the host or leader be intentional about connecting with each person as they enter the meeting space. If it is a church class environment, it is still recommended that the leader connect with each participant.

Refreshments and materials: In the small group, you can serve refreshments and facilitate fellowship between group members. In a class setting, talk with the attendees and ensure that they purchase all of their necessary materials (study guide and optional copy of *Preparing for the Glory*). Ideally, the small group members will have received all of their resources prior to Week 1, but if not, ensure that the materials are present at the meeting and available for group members to pick up or purchase.

Pray! Open every session in prayer, specifically addressing the topic that you will be covering in the upcoming meeting time. Invite the presence of the Holy Spirit to come, move among the group members and stir greater hunger in each participant to experience *more* of God's glory in their lives.

INTRODUCTIONS *(10 Minutes—First Class Only)*

Introduce yourself and allow each participant to briefly introduce him/herself. This should work fine for both small group and class environments. In a small group, you can go around the room and have each person introduce himself/herself one at a time. In a classroom setting, establish some type of flow and then have each person give a quick introduction (name, interesting fact, etc.).

Discuss the schedule for the meetings. Provide participants an overview of what the next eight weeks will look like. If you plan to do any type of social activities, you might want to advertise this right up front.

WORSHIP *(15 Minutes—Optional for the First Meeting)*

Fifteen minutes is a solid time for a worship segment. That said, it all depends upon the culture of your group. If everyone is okay with doing 30 minutes of praise and worship, by all means, go for it!

For this particular curriculum, a worship segment is highly recommended, as true and lasting transformation happens as we continually encounter God's presence.

PRAYER/MINISTRY TIME *(5–15 Minutes)*

At this point, you will transition from either welcome or worship into a time of prayer.

Just like praise and worship, it is recommended that this initial time of prayer be five to ten minutes in length; but if the group is made up of people who do not mind praying longer, it should not be discouraged. The key is stewarding everyone's time well while maintaining focus on the most important things at hand.

The prayer component is a time where group members will not just receive prayer, but also learn how to exercise Jesus' authority in their own lives and witness breakthrough in their circumstances.

After the door is opened through worship, the atmosphere is typically charged with God's presence.

TRANSITION TIME

At this point, you will transition from prayer/ministry time to watching the *Preparing for the Glory* DVDs.

Group leaders/class teachers: It is recommended that you have the DVD in the player and are all ready to press "play" on the appropriate session.

VIDEO/TEACHING *(20–25 Minutes)*

During this time, group members will answer the questions in their study guides and have a place to take notes.

SUMMARY

There is also short summary of the week's topic before the discussion questions. You can read this prior to the group meeting to provide you with a summary of that week's session.

DISCUSSION QUESTIONS *(20–30 Minutes)*

In the Leader's Guide there will be a number of questions to ask the group. Some questions will be phrased so you can ask them directly, others may have instructions or suggestions for how you can guide the discussion.

Some lessons will have more questions than others. Also, there might be some instances where you choose to cut out certain questions for the sake of time. This is entirely up to you, and in a circumstance where the Holy Spirit is moving and appears to be highlighting some questions more than others, flow in sync with the Holy Spirit. He will not steer you wrong!

As you ask the question in the group setting, encourage more than one person to provide an answer. Usually, you will have some people who are way off in their responses, but you will also have those who provide *part* of the correct answer.

Participants may feel like the conversation was lively, the dialogue insightful, and that the meeting was an overall success; but when all is said and done, the question, *"What do I do next?"* is not sufficiently answered. This is why every discussion time will be followed with an activation segment.

ACTIVATION (5–10 *Minutes*)

- Each activation segment should be five to ten minutes at the minimum, as this is the place where believers begin putting action to what they just learned.

- The activation segment will be custom-tailored for the session covered.

- Even though every group member might not be able to participate in the activation exercise, it gives them a visual for what it looks like to demonstrate the concept that they just studied.

PLANS FOR THE NEXT WEEK (2 *Minutes*)

Be sure to let group members know if the meeting location will change or differ from week to week, or if there are any other relevant announcements to your group/class. Weekly e-mails, Facebook updates, and text messages are great tools to communicate with your group. If your church has a database tool that allows for communication between small group/class leaders and members, that is an effective avenue for interaction as well.

CLOSE IN PRAYER

This is a good opportunity to ask for a volunteer to conclude the meeting with prayer.

Week 1

THE SUDDENLY OF GOD

JOURNAL

VIDEO LISTENING GUIDE

1. _____, _____, and _____ are examples of God working suddenly in the Bible.

2. A "suddenly" is a turn of _____ that changes your _____.

3. Jesus came in power suddenly after He spent 40 days in the _____.

4. We can't pay off our debt with _____. Instead, Jesus paid our debt with His _____.

5. Romans 8:28 says all things work unto _____ for those who _____ God.

Prayer Focus: Ask the Lord to help every participant 1) understand the importance of the power of faithfulness in their lives, and 2) learn how to steward breakthrough.

SUMMARY

Did you know the word "suddenly" is mentioned 72 times in scripture? That's because God often works in "suddenlies"—showing up and moving when we least expect it. Jesus Himself came as a suddenly. After the nation of Israel prayed for a Messiah, He *suddenly* came into the world in the most unexpected way: as a baby. This example and so many more reveal the heart of God to come into our lives and bring transformation.

This week's lesson focuses on how we can prepare our hearts for the suddenly of God. When we are aware of His heart to suddenly bring revival and power, we can be ready and equipped to steward His presence. One day soon, Jesus will come again in power for His bride. Are you ready for this—the greatest suddenly of all?

GOD'S HEART TO BRING BREAKTHROUGH

Of course, the Lord sometimes works gradually, teaching us about Himself over time. But many times, He comes when we least expect it, bringing about change and transformation. He loves us so much that He ordains times and experiences for us to encounter Him in this way!

PREPARE

Reflect

Review the following key concepts from John's teaching this week to prepare your heart and mind to lead. Take some time to journal through the ideas that stick out to you.

- "Suddenlies" are events in our lives where God changes our direction in an unexpected way.

- Many times God gives us prophetic clues as to when a "suddenly" will occur, but we have to be paying attention.

- Faithfulness means being prepared for the suddenly of God.

- Jesus will suddenly come for His bride, returning to establish a Kingdom of love, peace, joy on earth.

- God orchestrates "suddenlies" to bring breakthrough to His children.

Pause

Listen to God's heart for this week. Spend time in prayer asking the Lord what He wants to share with those in your group. Journal what you hear here. Make sure to include any ideas you have for your group time.

FELLOWSHIP, WELCOME, AND INTRODUCTIONS
(20-30 Minutes—For the First Meeting)

Welcome everyone as they walk in. If it is a small group environment, as the host or leader be intentional about connecting with each person as they come to the meeting space. If it is a church class environment, it is still recommended that the leader connects with each participant. However, there will be less pressure for the participants to feel connected immediately in a traditional class setting versus a more intimate small group environment.

In the small group, serve refreshments and facilitate fellowship between group members. In a class setting, talk with the attendees and ensure that they receive all of their necessary materials (the study guide and a copy of *Preparing for the Glory*).

Introduce yourself and allow participants to briefly introduce themselves as well. In a classroom setting, establish some type of flow and then have each person give a quick introduction (name, interesting fact, etc.).

Discuss the schedule for the meetings. Provide participants an overview of what the next eight weeks will look like and any potential social activities.

Distribute materials to each participant. Briefly orient the participants to the book and study guide, explaining the 15–20 minute time commitment for each day. Encourage each person to engage fully in this journey—they will get out of it only as much as they invest. This is a way to cultivate a habit of Bible study and daily time pursuing God's presence, starting with just 15–20 minutes. Morning, evening, afternoon—*when* does not matter.

OPENING PRAYER

WORSHIP *(15 Minutes—Optional for First Meeting)*

If a group chooses to do a worship segment, often they decide to begin on the second week. It usually takes an introductory meeting for everyone to become acquainted with one another and comfortable with their surroundings before they open up in worship.

PRAYER/MINISTRY TIME *(5–15 Minutes)*

VIDEO/TEACHING *(20 Minutes)*

DISCUSSION QUESTIONS *(25–30 Minutes)*

Spend some time dialoguing about the video content, covering the key concepts and talking points you prepared. Here are some possible questions you could use:

- What are some scriptural examples of God coming suddenly in an unexpected way?

- What does God's acting suddenly reveal about His heart or character?

- How can we be better prepared for the suddenly of God?

- How does knowing Jesus might return in our generation affect how we live?

Write down any questions that God puts on your heart.

What is the ultimate suddenly we are looking toward?

_____

_____

_____

_____

_____

_____

_____

_____

ACTIVATION: LEARN TO RECOGNIZE THE SUDDENLY OF GOD IN YOUR LIFE

Spend time in groups of two or three, and have your group members share about a time when God broke in suddenly.

How did this breakthrough compare to times when God worked more gradually or slowly?

What did God teach through His sudden work?

Have a couple of members share what God did for them and have them pray for the same grace to be released on the group.

CLOSE IN PRAYER

Thank you for leading a group in *Preparing the Glory*. We can't wait to see what the Lord does next week.

Week 2
THE BAPTISM OF FIRE, PART 1

JOURNAL

VIDEO LISTENING GUIDE

1. God gave us the Spirit to makes us more like _____ .

2. In the _____ of the Holy Spirit, the Lord imparts His boldness, presence, and _____ .

3. The Lord makes His ministers a _____ of _____ (see Psalm 104:4).

4. God's job in the miraculous is to _____ and our job is to _____ .

5. We are called to _____ the work He starts.

Prayer Focus: Ask the Lord to help every participant 1) understand the value for a baptism of fire by the Holy Spirit, and see the value for stewarding their own personal flame.

SUMMARY

In this session, Carol shares about what it means to be baptized in the fire of the Holy Spirit. When He comes upon us, He imparts His presence and power to us so we can live as Jesus lived. The good news is that there's even more of His fire to ignite us! Will we choose to live as a flame of fire for Him?

When we join with God in the work He is doing around us, we can grow in power and authority and bring revival to the world around us. As we see in Carol's example of praying over a young girl at church, choosing to partner with God in what He's already doing changes everything. It's His job to bring revival—all we have to do is walk with Him in it!

▌ PREPARE

Reflect

Review the following key concepts from Carol's teaching this week to prepare your heart and mind to lead. Take some time to journal through the ideas that stick out to you.

- The Spirit makes us more like Jesus.

- There is an impartation of more of God's presence, fire, and boldness in the baptism of the Holy Spirit.

- He makes His angels (ministers) a flame of fire (see Psalm 104:4).

- Don't give up when God does something powerful suddenly. Keep partnering with Him!

Pause

Listen to God's heart for this week. Spend time in prayer asking the Lord what He wants to share with those in your group. Journal what you hear here. Make sure to include any ideas you have for your group time.

FELLOWSHIP, WELCOME, AND INTRODUCTIONS
(20-30 Minutes—For the First Meeting)

Welcome everyone as they walk in. Be sure to identify any new members who were not at the previous session, and be sure that they receive the appropriate materials—study guide and book.

Encourage everyone to congregate in the meeting place. If it is a classroom setting, make an announcement that it is time to sit down and begin the session. If it is a small group, ensure everyone makes their way to the designated meeting space.

OPENING PRAYER

WORSHIP *(15-20 Minutes)*

PRAYER/MINISTRY TIME *(5–15 Minutes)*

VIDEO/TEACHING *(20 Minutes)*

DISCUSSION QUESTIONS *(25–30 Minutes)*

Spend some time dialoguing about the video content, covering the key concepts and talking points you prepared. Here are some possible questions you could use:

- What is the role of the Holy Spirit in our lives?

- What is the baptism of the Holy Spirit?

- What does it mean to be a "flame of fire" for God?

- In revival, what is God's job? What is our job?

- What happens when we partner with God in the work He's doing?

Write down any questions that God puts on your heart.

Psalm 104:4 tells us that God makes His ministers a flame of fire. When we live our lives before Him, postured in worship and ministry to His heart, He ignites us in His power.

ACTIVATION: BEING BAPTIZED IN THE HOLY SPIRIT

This will be a group exercise.

If possible, have praise and worship music ready to go—either live, or on some kind of audio system.

Have your group members share their experiences of being baptized in the Holy Spirit. What happened? What changes came in their lives as a result?

Some members might have experienced a baptism of the Holy Spirit, while others haven't yet had this experience. No matter the experience, God always wants to give us a fresh encounter.

Have a time of praise and worship. During this time pray for each other to experience to have a fresh baptism of the Holy Spirit.

CLOSE IN PRAYER

Great work! Now let's move on to week 3, where we will learn more about the baptism of the Holy Spirit.

Week 3
THE BAPTISM OF FIRE, PART 2

JOURNAL

VIDEO LISTENING GUIDE

1. On the day of Pentecost, Jesus sent His _____ _____.

2. Encountering God's _____ helps us grow in boldness.

3. Mark 7:21 says from _____ proceed evil thoughts.

4. The enemy wants to bring us back to a _____ level.

5. Zechariah 2:5 tells us God will be a _____ around us, the _____ in our midst.

Prayer Focus: Ask the Lord to help every participant 1) to have the presence soften any hard hearts, and renew the mind to carry God's glory in their own unique way.

SUMMARY

There are so many reasons to pursue the presence of God. Encounters with God ignite us with His fire. But when we soak in the Lord's love and come away with a new revelation of who He is, we empower the Holy Spirit to do meaningful work in our lives. From this place, we can step out in boldness with His fire on display to the world!

It's important to remember that the motivation of our pursuit matters. Many run toward the Lord for His power rather than out of love for Him, which doesn't yield the same results. Only when we direct our hearts toward Jesus in love will we bear the fruit of His power and presence.

Growing in Love for the Lord

Jesus wants us to run toward Him because we love Him, not just because of what we can get from Him. This means we need to focus on His character, not just His actions and gifts.

PREPARE

Reflect

Review the following key concepts from Carol's teaching this week to prepare your heart and mind to lead. Take some time to journal through the ideas that stick out to you.

- When we soak in God's presence, He softens our hearts.

- Our lives change when we allow our hearts to be radically in love with our Savior.

- Encountering God's love leads to empowering boldness.

- Your motivation in coming to God matters. When we use God for His power, we don't bear the same fruit.

- God's Spirit purifies us when we come to His presence.

Pause

Listen to God's heart for this week. Spend time in prayer asking the Lord what He wants to share with those in your group. Journal what you hear here. Make sure to include any ideas you have for your group time.

FELLOWSHIP, WELCOME, AND INTRODUCTIONS

Welcome everyone as they walk in. Be sure to identify any new members who were not at the previous session, and be sure that they receive the appropriate materials—study guide and book.

Encourage everyone to congregate in the meeting place. If it is a classroom setting, make an announcement that it is time to sit down and begin the session. If it is a small group, ensure everyone makes their way to the designated meeting space.

OPENING PRAYER

WORSHIP *(15-20 Minutes)*

PRAYER/MINISTRY TIME *(5–15 Minutes)*

VIDEO/TEACHING *(20 Minutes)*

DISCUSSION QUESTIONS *(25–30 Minutes)*

Spend some time dialoguing about the video content, covering the key concepts and talking points you prepared. Here are some possible questions you could use:

- How does God's love soften our hearts?

- Why is it important to have the right motive when running toward God?

- What does God say about being lukewarm?

- Why is it so important to identify the season you're in?

- What are the two aspects of God's fire?

Write down any questions that God puts on your heart.

The Lord's presence is a safe place for us to be transformed in Him. When we unite our hearts to His, He uproots unhealthy motivations and lies we believe so we can walk in wholeness.

ACTIVATION: THANKFULNESS FOR THE GLORY

This will be an individual exercise.

- If possible, have praise and worship music ready to go—either live, or on some kind of audio system.

- Spend time as individuals journaling and reflecting on the bush of fire that Moses encountered.

- Reflect on the "bushes of fire" they have seen in their own lives which are obvious signs of God's glory.

- How did this glory encounter change their heart and their lives?

After these things are identified and written down, have a time of praise and worship. This is a time to offer up thanksgiving to God, and prepare the way for more.

CLOSE IN PRAYER

Are you ready for next week? Join us as we learn about what it means to honor the anointing!

Week 4

HONORING THE ANOINTING

JOURNAL

VIDEO LISTENING GUIDE

1. The Word Messiah or Christ means "_____ _____."

2. John 6:63 says the Spirit gives _____ but the _____ profits nothing.

3. It's important to keep _____ accounts with God.

4. _____ means we can receive anointing from others.

5. The Spirit's power must never be separated from the Father's _____.

Prayer Focus: Ask the Lord to help every participant 1) to recognize the anointing that is in their life, and recognize the grace that is on the other members in the group.

SUMMARY

In the original Greek, the word "Christian" means "little anointed ones." As Christians, we carry God's anointing through the Holy Spirit. His work in us and through us isn't based on our merit. Still, it is crucial we learn to carry our anointing well, respecting it with how we live our daily lives. This is what it means to honor our anointing.

A Deeper Look at Our Anointing

The word "anointing" has an association with oil. In the Old Testament, Samuel anointed Kings Saul and David by putting oil on their heads. Anointing wasn't just a symbol, however. After they were anointed, Saul and David's identities were radically changed. In this way, anointing is an outward expression of a deeper inner transformation that takes place.

PREPARE

Reflect

Review the following key concepts from Carol's teaching this week to prepare your heart and mind to lead. Take some time to journal through the ideas that stick out to you.

- "Christian" means "little anointed one."

- The Spirit gives life; the flesh profits nothing (see John 6:63).

- We can receive anointing from others through the process of impartation.

- When Samuel anointed David and Saul, their hearts changed!

- If we don't have love with our anointing, we have nothing.

- The power and love of God go perfectly together.

Pause

Listen to God's heart for this week. Spend time in prayer asking the Lord what He wants to share with those in your group. Journal what you hear here. Make sure to include any ideas you have for your group time.

FELLOWSHIP, WELCOME, AND INTRODUCTIONS

Welcome everyone as they walk in. Be sure to identify any new members who were not at the previous session, and be sure that they receive the appropriate materials—study guide and book.

Encourage everyone to congregate in the meeting place. If it is a classroom setting, make an announcement that it is time to sit down and begin the session. If it is a small group, ensure everyone makes their way to the designated meeting space.

OPENING PRAYER

WORSHIP *(15-20 Minutes)*

PRAYER/MINISTRY TIME *(5–15 Minutes)*

VIDEO/TEACHING *(20 Minutes)*

DISCUSSION QUESTIONS *(25–30 Minutes)*

Spend some time dialoguing about the video content, covering the key concepts and talking points you prepared. Here are some possible questions you could use:

- What is significant about the image of oil when thinking about anointing?

- What does it mean that the "flesh profits nothing"?

- Why is it so important to have love in our anointing?

- What does it mean to impart something to someone?

- What is the relationship between God's power and love?

Write down any questions that God puts on your heart.

_____

_____

_____

_____

_____

_____

_____

The most profound way we can honor the anointing we carry is by investing love in everything we do.

ACTIVATION: HONORING THE ANOINTING

> *For I long to see you, that I may impart to you some spiritual gift to strengthen you—that is, that we may be mutually encouraged by each other's faith, both yours and mine* **(Romans 1:11-12 ESV).**

This will be a group exercise. Have the group break into groups of two or three. Have them take turns telling the other the grace and anointing that they see in the life of each other.

Then have each member pray over the group to impart that grace into one another's lives.

Have group members share how it felt to be honored publicly for what they carry.

CLOSE IN PRAYER

You're halfway through the course! God is doing powerful things in your heart and group, and we are praying for you as you lead.

Week 5
THE POWER OF HONOR

JOURNAL

VIDEO LISTENING GUIDE

1. Pure doctrine is rooted and _____ in love.

2. In Luke 4, Jesus reads from the book of _____ and announces His anointing. But people from His hometown did not see Him as _____.

3. _____ in the Old Testament was truthful about the fact He was anointed by God.

4. There is a difference between _____ and _____ about our anointing.

5. _____ almost missed the blessing of God.

Prayer Focus: Ask the Lord to help every participant 1) stay encouraged in the Lord, and recognize areas they might need to let go of bitterness and forgive someone.

SUMMARY

When Jesus read from Isaiah 61 in the temple, He went public with His anointing. But even as He performed great miracles and taught powerful messages of love, people didn't recognize Him as the Anointed One. In the same way, when we are anointed, others may not see us as God sees us.

It's so important for us as God's children to honor the anointing on others' lives and see people as God does. In the same way, we need not get discouraged or bitter when others don't recognize the anointing on our lives! While bitterness toward others can block the flow of the anointing, honor blesses us, others, and most of all, the Lord.

Grace Blockers

In the beginning of this week's teaching, John shares about "grace blockers," attitudes and behaviors that can block the flow of the anointing God has placed on us. Each one has a specific antidote that can release our anointing. For example, while telling a lie could block the flow of the anointing, honesty would be the antidote.

PREPARE

Reflect

Review the following key concepts from Carol's teaching this week to prepare your heart and mind to lead. Take some time to journal through the ideas that stick out to you.

- Certain attitudes or behaviors can block the grace of God in our lives.

- Pure doctrine is rooted and grounded in love.

- Jesus Himself was not recognized for His anointing, yet He did not grow bitter toward others.

- There is a difference between being boastful about your anointing and being honest about it.

- Seldom does God's way of doing things align with your expectations.

Pause

Listen to God's heart for this week. Spend time in prayer asking the Lord what He wants to share with those in your group. Journal what you hear here. Make sure to include any ideas you have for your group time.

FELLOWSHIP, WELCOME, AND INTRODUCTIONS

Welcome everyone as they walk in. Be sure to identify any new members who were not at the previous session, and be sure that they receive the appropriate materials—study guide and book.

Encourage everyone to congregate in the meeting place. If it is a classroom setting, make an announcement that it is time to sit down and begin the session. If it is a small group, ensure everyone makes their way to the designated meeting space.

OPENING PRAYER

WORSHIP (*15-20 Minutes*)

PRAYER/MINISTRY TIME (*5–15 Minutes*)

VIDEO/TEACHING (*20 Minutes*)

DISCUSSION QUESTIONS (*25–30 Minutes*)

Spend some time dialoguing about the video content, covering the key concepts and talking points you prepared. Here are some possible questions you could use:

- How can God's anointing be blocked?

- Why didn't Jesus get angry or bitter when others didn't recognize His anointing?

- What is the difference between boasting and being honest?

- Why do you think God calls us to humble work sometimes instead of keeping us in the spotlight?

- What is "pure doctrine"?

- What does God want as the foundation for all our beliefs/theology?

Write down any questions that God puts on your heart.

_____

_____

_____

_____

_____

Honor is the antidote to bitterness, a powerful way to protect our own anointing and celebrate others.

ACTIVATION: HONORING THE ANOINTING IN EACH OTHER

This will be a group exercise. Share with each other areas in life where you are needing grace in your life.

Have a member who has that grace in their life, pray for strength and grace to be released.

God has placed you in a community of people. Strengthen each other to step into the full promises of God.

CLOSE IN PRAYER

We believe God will honor the work you're doing to walk in your anointing! Good job this week—let's move on to week 6!

Week 6
WALKING IN HOLINESS

JOURNAL

VIDEO LISTENING GUIDE

1. God does not want us to take His _____ for granted.

2. The next cloud of glory God brings will be a cloud of _____.

3. The _____ of the Lord is the beginning of wisdom.

4. If we want to see revival, God calls us to walk in _____.

5. Jesus said, "I only _____ what I hear my Father _____. I only _____ what I hear Him _____.

Prayer Focus: Ask the Lord to help every participant to awaken to the need for holiness in our lives, and step into new levels of obedience to His calling.

SUMMARY

God's grace is a wonderful gift to us. But when we focus on His graciousness, it can be easy to lose sight of His holiness. In this teaching, Carol invites us to awaken to the Lord's holiness and allow it to bring us to a place of repentance. When we humble ourselves before Him in obedience and refuse to compromise our character, we will see the signs, wonders, and revivals we have prayed for!

Thoughts on Holiness

Carol had a dream in which the Lord reveals the powerful effect of small decisions we make in our daily lives. While it may seem like our little compromises don't make a big difference, they actually grieve the heart of God and impact our relationship with Him. They can even keep us from encountering the revival we contend for.

PREPARE

Reflect

Review the following key concepts from Carol's teaching this week to prepare your heart and mind to lead. Take some time to journal through the ideas that stick out to you.

- The Lord sometimes tests our obedience.

- Some of us take God's grace for granted, but He's calling us to a new level of holiness.

- God is giving us a chance to repent and turn away from areas of compromise in our lives.

- If we want to move in signs and wonders, it's crucial that we walk in obedience.

- The holiness the Lord is calling us to is an inward holiness based in His love.

Pause

Listen to God's heart for this week. Spend time in prayer asking the Lord what He wants to share with those in your group. Journal what you hear here. Make sure to include any ideas you have for your group time.

FELLOWSHIP, WELCOME, AND INTRODUCTIONS

Welcome everyone as they walk in. Be sure to identify any new members who were not at the previous session, and be sure that they receive the appropriate materials—study guide and book.

Encourage everyone to congregate in the meeting place. If it is a classroom setting, make an announcement that it is time to sit down and begin the session. If it is a small group, ensure everyone makes their way to the designated meeting space.

OPENING PRAYER

WORSHIP *(15-20 Minutes)*

PRAYER/MINISTRY TIME *(5–15 Minutes)*

VIDEO/TEACHING *(20 Minutes)*

DISCUSSION QUESTIONS *(25-30 Minutes)*

Spend some time dialoguing about the video content, covering the key concepts and talking points you prepared. Here are some possible questions you could use:

- What does it mean to fear the Lord? How is this fear different from being afraid?

- How does fearing God lead to wisdom?

- What role does wisdom play in holiness?

- Why is it so important to pursue holiness?

- How does God respond to us when we repent?

Write down any questions that God puts on your heart.

The fear of the Lord is the beginning of wisdom (Proverbs 9:10).

ACTIVATION: HOLINESS AND GRACE

Individually, take time to reflect on God's holiness and grace. Journal about which of those two you have focused on more in the past and ask God for a fresh perspective on the one you feel less confident in.

Share with the group about where you are needing to grow and develop more insight.

After each member shares, pray for them to step into new levels of seeing God's holiness and grace.

Encourage the people you pray for to actively go after developing this deeper realization throughout the week.

CLOSE IN PRAYER

Week 6 is complete! Move forward in power and confidence, knowing God sees you as pure and beloved! You're doing a great job leading your group.

Week 7

STEWARDING THE ANOINTING

JOURNAL

VIDEO LISTENING GUIDE

1. It's important to have a _____ model in place to sustain the anointing.

2. _____ will go until revival leaders get worn out and carry on.

3. Take God on His _____, not on yours.

4. The book of _____ saw the greatest revival of all time.

5. God wants us to _____ revival, not _____ it.

Prayer Focus: Ask the Lord to help every participant 1) take responsibility for the anointing in their own life, and discover tools to co-labor with the Lord.

SUMMARY

Stewarding the anointing means sustaining the fire of God. Rather than a one-time encounter, we can walk in a lifestyle of signs and wonders, boldly stepping into the power of God each day. In this interview session, John and Carol share powerful truths and practical insights from their experience on hosting God's presence and fanning the flame of revival wherever you are.

When we take responsibility over the anointing the Lord has brought, He is faithful! Let's work together with Him to sustain what He's started.

Creating a Culture of Revival

Think of stewarding the anointing as creating a revival culture. With the right tools and plans in place, you can co-labor with the Lord to keep the fire burning in your ministry, church, or home.

▌ PREPARE

Reflect

Review the following key concepts from Carol's teaching this week to prepare your heart and mind to lead. Take some time to journal through the ideas that stick out to you.

- Revival isn't just a one-time experience. We want it to grow and multiply.

- Having a team model in place can be an important way to steward the anointing.

- If you want to see revival grow, take God on His terms, not on your terms.

- God is wiser than we are, and He will do things how they need to be done. Join with what He's doing. Invite the Spirit to come in.

- To find out if what you're experiencing is of the Lord, ask "Is Jesus being glorified? Is the fruit good?"

Pause

Listen to God's heart for this week. Spend time in prayer asking the Lord what He wants to share with those in your group. Journal what you hear here. Make sure to include any ideas you have for your group time.

FELLOWSHIP, WELCOME, AND INTRODUCTIONS

Welcome everyone as they walk in. Be sure to identify any new members who were not at the previous session, and be sure that they receive the appropriate materials—study guide and book.

Encourage everyone to congregate in the meeting place. If it is a classroom setting, make an announcement that it is time to sit down and begin the session. If it is a small group, ensure everyone makes their way to the designated meeting space.

OPENING PRAYER

WORSHIP *(15-20 Minutes)*

PRAYER/MINISTRY TIME *(5–15 Minutes)*

VIDEO/TEACHING *(20 Minutes)*

DISCUSSION QUESTIONS *(25–30 Minutes)*

Spend some time dialoguing about the video content, covering the key concepts and talking points you prepared. Here are some possible questions you could use:

- How is preparing for the anointing a way of stewarding the anointing?

- Why is having a team in place so crucial?

- Is it okay to ask God questions? What is the fruit of asking God questions?

- Why does God sometimes ask us to go places with Him that "offend our minds"?

- What does it mean to partner with God in what He's doing?

Write down any questions that God puts on your heart.

_____

_____

_____

_____

_____

_____

_____

_____

_____

_____

_____

_____

_____

_____

_____

Let a man regard us in this manner, as servants of Christ and stewards of the mysteries of God (1 Corinthians 4:1 NASB).

ACTIVATION: HONORING THE ANOINTING IN EACH OTHER

This is a group exercise. Have each person read Acts 2 at Pentecost and write down what were the roots and the fruits of revival.

What was the root (cause) of this revival? What was the fruit (result) of it?

Pray together for the Spirit to move in a similar way in your life.

CLOSE IN PRAYER

We hope you are encouraged! We have one more week together. Let's prepare our hearts to receive what the Lord wants to say and do.

Week 8
RELEASING THE ANOINTING

JOURNAL

VIDEO LISTENING GUIDE

1. God wants us to bring the anointing to the seven _____ of culture.

2. Pastoring anointing is different than trying to _____ it.

3. Giving God our _____ time will always bear fruit.

4. Sometimes, all we have to do is open our _____ and be _____ to release the anointing.

5. God wants to see His _____ released in our spheres of influence!

Prayer Focus: Ask the Lord to help every participant 1) have a vision for their sphere of influence, and recognize their responsibility to pastor and shepherd revival in their own personal life.

SUMMARY

In this final session, John and Carol take time to pray for leaders looking for revival strategy and offer crucial insight on what it means to pastor the anointing. As we keep in step with the Spirit, He will give us the tools we need to sustain a culture of revival wherever we are, and just as importantly, bring it out into the world. Partnered with Him and plugged into the Lord's love, nothing is impossible for us!

Pastoring the Anointing

If we want the anointing to thrive and grow, it's important to be intentional and strategic. Rather than following our own whims, God wants us to partner with the work of the Spirit and respond to Him.

PREPARE

Reflect

Review the following key concepts from Carol's teaching this week to prepare your heart and mind to lead. Take some time to journal through the ideas that stick out to you.

- To steward and release our anointing, it's important to pastor it, not control it.

- Taking time to meet with God regularly will always bear fruit.

- God wants our encounters with Him to shift the rest of our lives.

- We get to step out in faithfulness and release His glory wherever we go.

- The Lord is waiting to work and heal through us.

Pause

Listen to God's heart for this week. Spend time in prayer asking the Lord what He wants to share with those in your group. Journal what you hear here. Make sure to include any ideas you have for your group time.

FELLOWSHIP, WELCOME, AND INTRODUCTIONS

Welcome everyone as they walk in.

Encourage everyone to congregate in the meeting place. If it is a classroom setting, make an announcement that it is time to sit down and begin the session. If it is a small group, ensure everyone makes their way to the designated meeting space.

OPENING PRAYER

WORSHIP (*15-20 Minutes*)

PRAYER/MINISTRY TIME (*5–15 Minutes*)

VIDEO/TEACHING (*20 Minutes*)

DISCUSSION QUESTIONS (*25–30 Minutes*)

Spend some time dialoguing about the video content, covering the key concepts and talking points you prepared. Here are some possible questions you could use:

- How can spending time with the Lord equip us to release our anointing?

- What happens when we let the Spirit lead instead of trying to control things?

- What is the difference between being strategic and controlling a situation?

- Why is it so important for the revival we experience at church to go beyond the four walls of the building?

- What is the relationship between personal and corporate revival?

Write down any questions that God puts on your heart.

_____

_____

_____

_____

_____

_____

_____

_____

_____

_____

_____

_____

Now the God of peace...equip you in every good thing to do His will, working in us that which is pleasing in His sight, through Jesus Christ, to whom be the glory forever and ever. Amen (Hebrews 13:20-21 NASB).

ACTIVATION: SPHERES OF INFLUENCE

This will be a group exercise. Gather in groups of two. Have each participant share the areas where they feel like they are supposed to influence and effect.

Spend time praying over one another. Ask the Lord for wisdom on how to release the anointing in your individual sphere of influence and pray over your partner for grace to release theirs.

Take time to pray corporately, for a greater anointing for perseverance, strength, and the ability to press on. This is key to spiritual maturity, particularly for those desiring to walk in the supernatural life.

PLANS FOR THE NEXT WEEK

Let participants know that either this is the final week of the study or that you will be having some type of social activity on the following week—or at a specified future date.

CLOSE IN PRAYER

Pray that the group would truly be able to strengthen themselves in the Lord as they continue to daily walk out the tools that have been presented throughout the course.

Thank you so much for joining us for the last eight weeks. We are so encouraged and blessed by your commitment to prepare for the coming glory of God. We will be praying for you as you seek Him and share His love with the world.

ABOUT
JOHN AND CAROL ARNOTT

John and Carol Arnott are the founding pastors of Catch the Fire—formerly known as the Toronto Airport Christian Fellowship—and overseers of the Partners in Harvest Network of Churches. As international speakers, John and Carol have become known for their ministry of revival in the context of the Father's saving and restoring love. As the Holy Spirit moves with signs and wonders, they have seen millions of lives touched and changed through God's power and Christ's love.

FREE E-BOOKS?
YES, PLEASE!

Get **FREE** and deeply-discounted **Christian books** for your **e-reader** delivered to your inbox **every week!**

IT'S SIMPLE!

VISIT lovetoreadclub.com

SUBSCRIBE by entering your email address

RECEIVE free and discounted e-book offers and inspiring articles delivered to your inbox every week!

Unsubscribe at any time.

SUBSCRIBE NOW!

LOVE TO READ CLUB

visit **LOVETOREADCLUB.COM** ▶

JOURNAL

JOURNAL

JOURNAL

JOURNAL

JOURNAL

JOURNAL

JOURNAL

JOURNAL

JOURNAL

JOURNAL

Made in the USA
Columbia, SC
11 December 2022